Hearty & Free Publishing
EST. 2021

Copyright © 2023
Jennifer Smith and Katie Larabee

All rights reserved. No part of this book may be reproduced in any form without permission in writing from the author. Reviewers may quote brief passages in reviews.

Disclaimer

Copyright notice: All rights reserved under the International and Pan-American Copyright Conventions. No part of this book may be reproduced or transmitted in any form or by any means, electronic or mechanical, including photocopying and recording, or by any information storage and retrieval system, without permission in writing from publisher.

The advice and strategies found within may not be suitable for every situation. This work is sold with the understanding that neither the author nor the publisher are held responsible for the results accrued from the advice in this book.

Warning: the unauthorized reproduction or distribution of this copyrighted work is illegal. Criminal copyright infringement, including infringement without monetary gain, is investigated by the FBI and is punishable by up to 5 years in prison and a fine of $250,000.

For more information, email support@heartyandfree.com

Library of Congress Control Number: 2023916126

Paperback ISBN: 979-8-9889430-0-6
Hardcover ISBN: 979-8-9889430-1-3
eBook ISBN: 979-8-9889430-2-0

Cover Design: Katie Larabee

Dedication ♡ ♡

To Skyler, you are my sunshine.
To Aunt Carla, for believing in
the Adventure.

♡ ♡ Thank you ♡ ♡

Gran and Pa, for getting me to
adulthood and doing it so well.

Jourdan, for the realization that
I am a creative soul.

Wild Awakening Sisters,
for the encouragement to
do the dang thing.

Stell, for inspiring me to explore
the arts.

David & Family, for the flow of love.

TAP IT OUT

The Adventures of BABY STAR

Written by:
Jennifer Smith

Illustrated by:
Katie Larabee

Hi there!
My name is Baby Star.

Have you ever wondered what you can do to help with your feelings of anger, sadness, frustration, or embarrassment?

FRUSTRATION

EMBARASMENT

ANGER

SADNESS

Have you ever been so **Sad** you wanted to cry, but didn't really know why?

Or weren't somewhere you felt comfortable to cry it out?

Have you ever been so **Mad** you wanted to punch or throw something, but you couldn't?

Have you ever been so **Frustrated** you wanted to scream, but were told not to be so loud?

Have you ever been so **Embarrassed** you wanted to hide in a corner and never come out?

Yeah,
I've been there.

And luckily, I have found a way that helps
me through ALL of my emotions...
...and even those I don't understand.

4

TAPPING!

No, no, no.
Not the kind you put the loud shoes on and tap your feet on the ground with.

This kind of tapping is actually much much quieter. (And it feels better too.)

This will help no matter where you are. In a car, in class, in your bedroom, and even at the dentist.

Let me show you how.

6

The first thing
to do is...
find these points
on your body.

Top of your Head

Between and only slightly
above your Eyebrows

Side of your Eye

Under your Eye

Under your Nose

On your Chin

Right below the inner
points of your Collarbone

And slightly below
your Underarm

Get Comfortable. Get ready to try it out!

On the floor, on the couch, in a chair, or even on your bed.

Tap each point several times.

Start with the top of your head and work your way down under your arm.

The first few times you might feel silly and
not want to talk about how you are feeling.

And that's ok!

You will notice just by tapping, your attitude toward whatever
emotion you are feeling begins to change.

And that is good!

Just by gently tapping these points on your body
you will do wonders to help yourself feel better.

It's almost like magic!

Now that you know the points, let's try it again.

As you tap each spot, all you have to do is start talking out loud about how you feel.

Why do you feel that way?

What would make you feel better?

What does this feeling bring up for you?
Sad? Feeling bad? Frustrated?

Then don't forget to tell yourself how awesome and amazing you are.

Some feelings might need more tapping than others. It could take one minute, or it could take lots more.

Keep talking through your feelings and tapping the areas until you have tapped it all out.

And if you're in a safe place, you might even want to cry or scream or rage. And that is ok!

Go ahead and try it when you are ready.
What are you feeling right now?

frustrated?

Sad?

Angry?

Annoyed?

Embarrassed?

As you sit thinking about how you are feeling,
does anything make it better or worse?

Lean into that change and
start talking about it and tapping it out.

Nothing you say or feel is ever wrong.

Did you notice a change yet in your feelings?

If not, that is ok, you are still learning.

Remind yourself it will get better.

This is where you get to be authentically you, raw emotions and everything.

Keep going.
You've got this!

Hey Parents!

Sometimes everything we do to try and help our children through tough times and emotions just doesn't seem to do the trick. Tapping is a way to allow your child to self-soothe and work through their emotions on their own. Who knows, you might even want to try tapping for yourself. The first few times (or more) you will want to do it with them. You will want to prompt them on what to say and where to tap. I have included examples here at the end of the book. There are also blank pages if you would like to make notes or journal your experiences.

I have been tapping with my five year old daughter for a while now. I have noticed how quickly she is able to work through her anger, fear, and anxiety when we tap it out versus when we do nothing. At her age, she may not understand what is happening, but it DOES help her on an energetic level to feel a positive change. When she gets older she will better understand what she is saying and feeling.

If you would like more information on tapping, please visit our website at www.tapitoutbook.com You will find more examples, prompts, and techniques. Also feel free to leave your feedback, questions, and what you would like to hear about next, as I will continue creating more books on how to help kids set themselves free.

I truly hope this helps you and your child.

So much love to you,

♡ Jennifer

Your turn! Find the points to tap on Baby Bear.

You are in control.
Some points may be tender or feel electric.
You may want to tap on those spots longer.
You've got this!

Angry feelings example

- **I feel angry.**
- Sooo angry.
- And I don't like it!
- Why did I not get invited to the party?
- Why couldn't Maggie just invite me?
- I thought I was her friend!
- I'm so angry!
- I'm a good person, right?
- I deserve to be there. I invited her to my party, why couldn't she invite me back to hers?
- Maybe I will ask her why. Maybe she just forgot?
- But if she forgot about me, maybe we aren't really friends like I thought.
- I feel like nobody likes me. Maybe they're talking behind my back about me at this party.
- I will talk to her tomorrow and share what's on my heart. That's all I can do.
- And if she doesn't really think I am a friend, at least I will know.

- Because deep down,
- I know that I am amazing
- And I deserve to be happy and have friends who love me.
- Because I'm amazing
- And I know that what I think of me is most important.
- Other people can have their own opinions about me
- And it means NOTHING about me
- I just have to like me
- I like me
- I think I'm pretty cool
- **I'm awesome!**

16

Sad feelings example

- **My dog died today.**

- It was really sad to say goodbye.
- Why did this have to happen?
- This isn't fair!
- I loved him so much.
- He was a big part our family.
- I'm gonna miss him a lot.
- It's gonna be weird to come home now and him not be there.
- Who am I going to cuddle with now?
- I feel like a piece of my heart is missing.
- This is really tough.
- I want to scream. I just want to cry for days and days.
- I'm going to let myself be sad.
- And then talk to my mom and see if there's something we can do to honor him.
- I miss my best friend.

- For now I'm going to allow myself to feel these sad feelings.
- It's okay to cry.
- It's okay to be mad and angry that he got sick and couldn't be here longer.
- All of my feelings are valid.
- This is gonna take awhile to move through, and that's okay.

- **I give myself space to feel my sadness.**
- **And if I need a hug, I'll ask for one.**

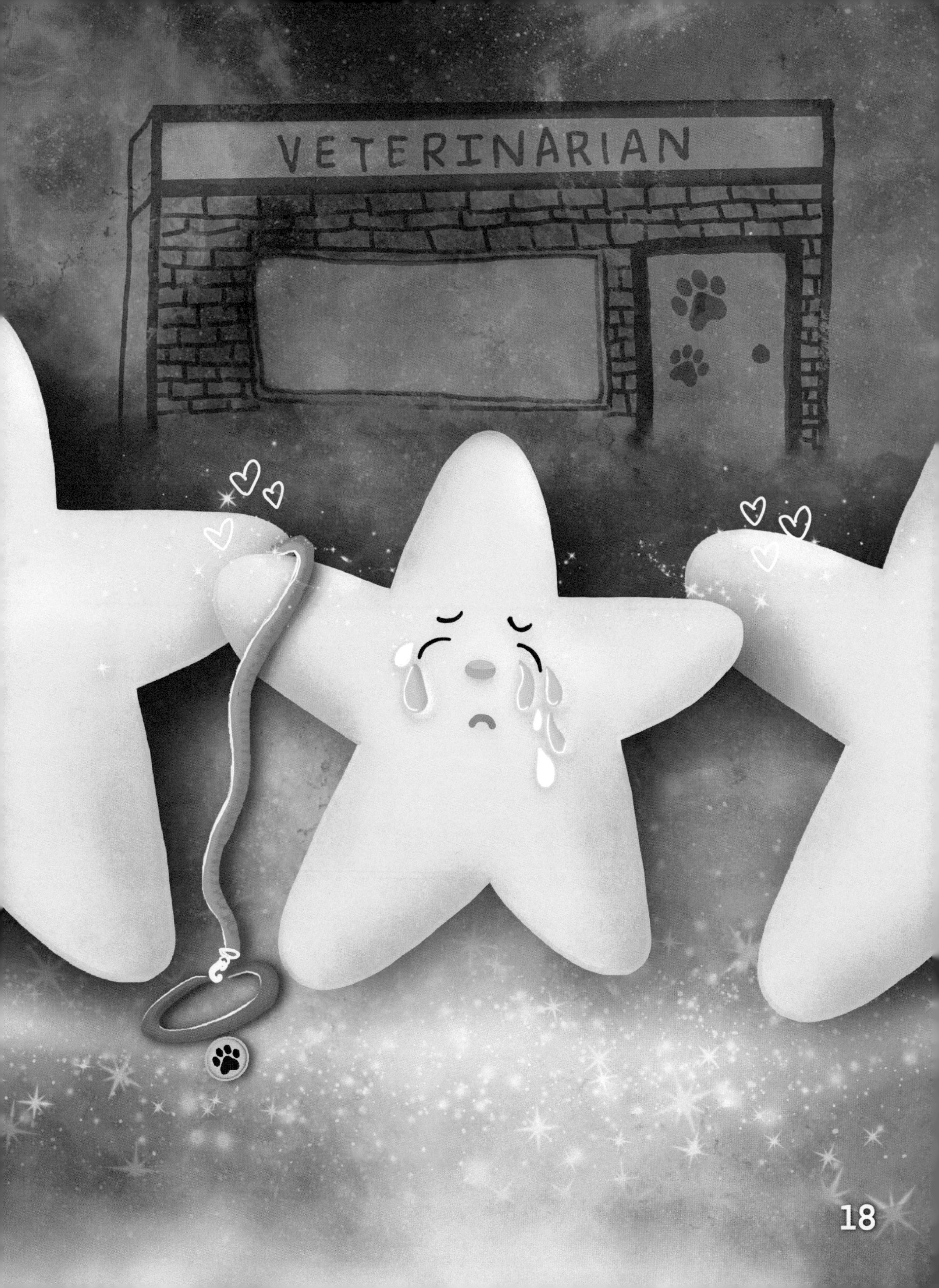
VETERINARIAN

Embarrassed feelings example

- Oh my goodness!

- I sneezed and tooted at the same time!

- I am sooo embarrassed.
- I want to run away and hide.
- Everyone is laughing at me.
- I wish I could crawl into a corner and never come out.
- Why did I have to do that in front of everyone? Even my best friend is laughing at me.
- Oh gosh, why couldn't I have gone and done that in the bathroom?
- What is wrong with me? Why couldn't I hold that in?
- I didn't know it would come out right then. I could cry I'm so embarrassed. But then they'll laugh at me more for crying.

- I'm allowed to have accidents, right?
- Everybody toots.
- Mine just came out loudly. Ha!
- I wish everyone wouldn't have laughed.
- But oh well, it happened.
- And I can't change what happened.
- But what I can change is allowing myself to feel these uncomfortable, embarrassed feelings, and let them flow though.
- Just like a toot! Ha, that's actually funny.
- I am human.
- And I am allowed to make mistakes and have accidents.

- I'm okay. I've got this.

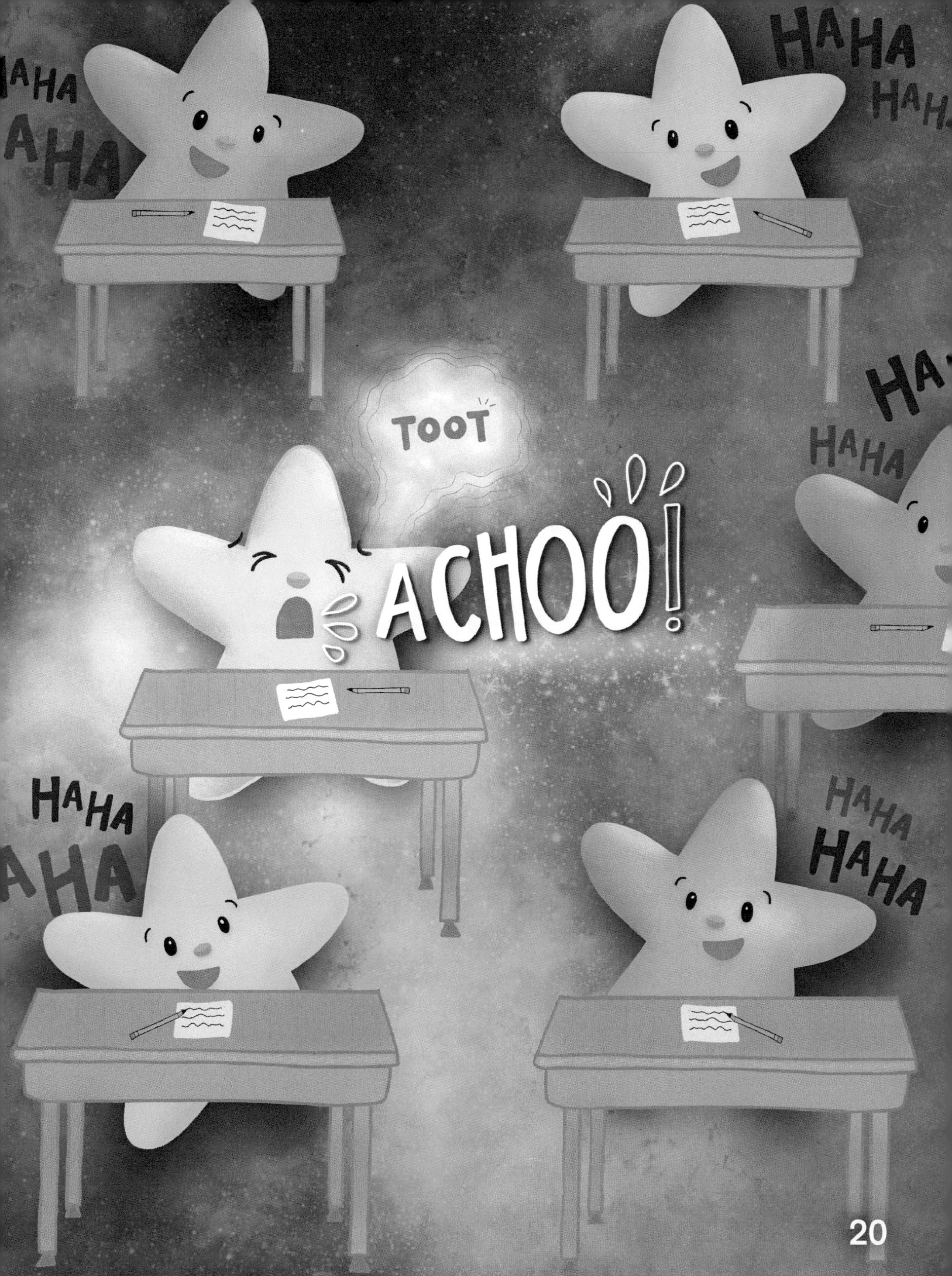
HAHA
HAHA
HAHA
HAHA
HA
HAHA
TOOT
ACHOO!
HAHA
HAHA
HAHA
HAHA

Notes

Use this section to make notes
(or even draw pictures if you want).

What helps you when you tap?
Being in the dark?
Sitting in silence?
Laying down?

What triggers your emotions?
Is it always at school?
Is it always a certain person?
Is it always a certain time of day?
What makes you feel out of balance?
What makes you feel better?

Tapping, of course!
But what about a walk with your dog? Or coloring?

Or singing your favorite song at the top of your lungs?
Talk to your parents about how you feel.
Do more of these things.

I can't wait to hear how you are doing.
Visit our website and let me know how
tapping has helped you!

♡ Loving all of you,